WRESTLING

Mike Wilson

Published in association with The Basic Skills Agency

Hodder & Stoughton

A MEMBER OF THE HODDER HEADLINE GROUP

Acknowledgements
Cover: Will Hart/Allsport, Getty Images.

Photos: p. iv © Mary Evans picture library; p. 6 © to come; p. 12 © SPP/Rex Features; p. 17 © Dave Allocca/Rex Features; p. 19 © Norm Betts/Rex Features; p. 22 © Universal/Everett/Rex Features; p. 25 © Anny Chettleborough/Rex Features.

Every effort has been made to trace copyright holders of material reproduced in this book. Any rights not acknowledged will be acknowledged in subsequent printings if notice is given to the publisher.

Orders; please contact Bookpoint Ltd, 130 Milton Park, Abingdon, Oxon OX14 4SB. Telephone (44) 01235 827720, Fax: (44) 01235 400454. Lines are open from 9.00–6.00, Monday to Saturday, with a 24 hour message answering service. You can also order through our website www.hodderheadline.co.uk

British Library Cataloguing in Publication Data
A catalogue record for this title is available from the British Library

ISBN 0 340 87142 3

First published 2003
Impression number   10 9 8 7 6 5 4 3 2 1
Year   2007 2006 2005 2004 2003

Typeset by SX Composing DTP, Rayleigh, Essex.
Printed in Great Britain for Hodder & Stoughton Educational, a division of Hodder Headline, 338 Euston Road, London NW1 3BH by The Bath Press, Bath.

Contents

Wrestling.

Wrestling in the 14th century.

1 The Oldest Sport in the World

Wrestling is the oldest sport in the world.

Thousands of years ago,
Greeks and Romans wrestled.
Africans and North American Indians wrestled.

Richard the Lionheart,
King of England (1157–1199)
was a wrestler.

So was King Henry the Eighth (1491–1547).

So was Abraham Lincoln
(President of the USA from 1860 to 1865).

But when wrestling went professional,
it stopped being a sport.
It became entertainment.

The oldest sport in the world
would never be the same again.

2 Wrestling Rules

Wrestling has a history
in every part of the world.
And in every part of the world,
the rules of wrestling are slightly different.

In Ancient Rome,
you put oil on your body
to make it harder to pinch the skin,
or get a hold.

Nowadays,
it's illegal to put oil or grease
on your body.

In the Greek and Roman rules –
that some still apply today –
you must not hold below the waist.

In America,
wrestling is more 'freestyle'.
Holds below the waist
and holds round the neck
are both okay.

In most places,
wrestlers had to have bare feet,
but in Devon,
they used to wear big boots
with steel plates in the soles.
They'd kick each other's shins
until the boots were full of blood!

In Cumbria,
the match can't start
until you've both got a good grip.
You clasp your hands together
behind the other man's back.
Then – without letting go –
you both start trying
to force each other to the ground.

In the Greek and Roman style,
you only lost a match
if both your shoulders touched the ground.
But in other styles,
you lost if you touched the ground
with *any* part of your body –
except your hands, feet and knees.

Or you lost if one shoulder and one foot
touched the ground.
Or one shoulder, two hips.
Or two shoulders, one hip . . .

Some of the rules were a bit clearer:

• no kicking
• no punching
• no elbowing
• no strangling
• no poking in the eye
• no pulling hair
• no biting
• no spitting
• no throwing out of the ring
• no hitting the referee
• no hitting the people in the crowd.

3 The First Wrestling Star

Frank Gotch was the first wrestling star,
the best all-round wrestler
the world had ever seen.

By the time he retired in 1913,
Frank Gotch was a star.
He was also a very rich man.

Wrestling was big business in those days.
Frank Gotch had met the US President many times,
and starred in a hit stage-play.

One day, thousands of people gathered
when they spotted Frank chatting on the street.
Mounted police had to break up the crowds.

Crowds gathered to watch wresting around the time of Frank Gotch's
fame.

Frank Gotch came from the state of Iowa in the USA.
In 1901, when he was just 19 years old
Frank spent six months wrestling for money
in the mining towns of Alaska.
He went home with $30,000 –
a fortune in those days.

He then toured the USA,
looking for men to wrestle.
He never lost a match.

For one of his matches,
with a wrestler called The Russian Lion,
the crowd was nearly 30,000 strong!

The problem with that fight was –
it was actually pretty boring.
Unless you were a total wrestling fan.

Frank Gotch and The Russian Lion
fought for two hours solid –
two experts, very skilled, very strong,
and very patient.
They held on to each other for ages,
careful not to give anything away.
It was not fun to watch.

4 Sport or Show-biz?

The fans were paying for entertainment.
So managers made sure they got it.

By the 1930s, wrestling was exciting.
Wrestling was non-stop action.
Wrestling was larger than life.

Not all wrestlers liked it.
'It wasn't sport any more,' said one.
'It was just show-biz – just like it is today.'

Another one said, 'I'd go out there and wrestle.
I'd get the other guy, so he couldn't move.
But then I'd have to let him go.
The fans would wonder how he got out of that . . .'

The real wrestlers soon went back
to the amateur game.

They left the glory and the big money
to the showmen.

5 Wrestling Stars in the UK

In the UK, wrestling was put on TV in 1955.

Soon millions were watching
every Saturday afternoon.
Even the Queen became a fan.

Top wrestlers became rich celebrities.

There was Mick McManus.
He had a lot of respect as a wrestler,
but he was the one the fans loved to hate.

There was Kendo Nagasaki.
He dressed as a Japanese warrior
and always wore a mask.
Nobody knew who he was.

Then there was Giant Haystacks.
He was over forty stone.
He was Kendo Nagasaki's number one enemy.

It was Giant Haystacks
who pulled off his mask in one fight.
Underneath was Peter Thornley.
Kendo Nagasaki wasn't Japanese at all!

Then there was Jackie Pallo.

Jackie Pallo took the mask off British wrestling.
He wrote a book called *You Grunt, I'll Groan.*

It said that the wrestling game was all fixed.
You got instructions –
who would lose, who would win,
what round it would be in . . .

Jackie Pallo said it was all for show.

Jackie was always popular with the fans.
But after he wrote his book,
he was not popular with other wrestlers.
He found it hard to get work,
and retired soon after – aged 58.

'The death of wrestling,' he said.
'It started the day I retired.'

6 Big Daddy

Other people blame Big Daddy
for the death of wrestling.

Big Daddy was not a good wrestler,
but his manager – his brother –
made sure he always won.

The trouble was
Big Daddy was big – too big.
He was good fun,
but he wasn't very fit.
He couldn't wrestle for long,
so his fights all had to end quickly.

Big Daddy's fights were good for a laugh.
But where was the excitement?

Big Daddy.

7 Wrestling is Sexy!

All the excitement was in America.

By the 1990s,
crowds of over 20,000 people
were going to see wrestling –
just like in the good old days.

In the UK,
Big Daddy was a big hit on kids' TV.
He was over twenty stone.

In America,
wrestlers looked lean and mean.
Wrestlers were fit and strong.
Wrestlers were good-looking.

In America, wrestling was sexy.

In America,
there were Hardcore Fights.
(No holds barred.
Anything goes.)

In America,
there were Battle Royal Fights.
(You won when you threw the other guy
out of the ring.)

In America,
there were Ambulance Fights.
(You won when you threw the other guy
into an ambulance.)

In America,
women were joining in too.
Taking on the men
at their own game.

8 Vince McMahon

The story of American wrestling
is the story of Vince McMahon.

He was born in the USA in 1945.
As a kid, he never knew his dad.
He lived with his mom in a mobile home.
He was beaten and abused.
It made him tough.

After he left school,
Vince worked with his dad.
His dad put on wrestling matches.
Soon Vince knew wrestling was his life.

In 1982, Vince was ready to take over the world.
He began the World Wrestling Federation (WWF).
Under Vince fights got bigger.
Wrestlers became megastars, Vince McMahon
became very rich.

Crowds got bigger.
Money poured in.

For ten years, Vince had it all his way.
But in 1992, Vince was in court.
Some of his wrestlers had been taking drugs.
Illegal body-building drugs.
They said they'd got the drugs from Vince.

Vince was found not guilty
but he had to stay out of wrestling for two years.
When the two years were up,
the WWF was dead in the water.

Ted Turner was running the show now.
Ted Turner owned the news network CNN.
Now he wanted to own American wrestling as well.

Vince had to fight back.
He put on fights that were rougher, and tougher,
than ever before.

WWF wrestlers became extreme.

Vince McMahon.

They fought dirty.
They swore.
They got mad at each other –
in the ring and out of it.
WWF wrestlers were more grown up.
Soon, the fans were more grown up too.

Wrestling had been a sport for kids to watch.
Now it was a man's game.

9 From 'The Hulk' to 'The Rock'

The first WWF megastar was Hulk Hogan.
He wasn't the best wrestler in the world,
but he was a real showman.

He got his name – and his first big break –
from Vince McMahon's dad.

The Hulk was the star of the first big
WrestleMania event in 1985.

For the next eight years,
no one could touch him.

In Wrestlemania 2, Hulk beat King Kong Bundy.
He pulled Bundy's manager into the ring
and gave him a beating too!

Then he beat Andre the Giant in
Wrestlemania 3.

Hulk Hogan.

Andre the Giant was seven foot four.
But the Hulk still picked him up
and smashed him to the canvas!

Hulk beat everyone there was to beat.
He was World Champion
a record five times in eight years.

He also still found time to star in pop videos,
and a lot of movies like *Rocky 3*, *Gremlins 2*,
Suburban Commando and *Mr. Nanny*.

When Hulk Hogan retired,
there was a gap at the top of world wrestling.

'Stunning' Steve Austin filled that gap.
But only after a name-change.

'Stunning' Steve became 'Stone Cold'.
He became mean and merciless.
No more Mr Nice Guy.

The fans loved it.
'Stone Cold' was the man to beat
for the next few years.

In 2002, 'Stone Cold' was in trouble.
He fell out with Vince McMahon.
He walked out of the WWF.
And he fell out with his wife,
wrestling diva, Debra.

Debra had to call the police one night.
'Stone Cold' had hit her in anger.

'Stone Cold' was out in the cold
and 'The Rock' became the next Mr Popular.

Dwayne Johnson
had been an American Football player,
but he came from a family of wrestlers –
from Samoa in the South Pacific.

Like Steve Austin,
he changed his name on the way to the top.

Dwayne Johnson
became Rocky Maivia.
Rocky Maivia
became 'The Rock'.

'The Rock'.

'The Rock' has the respect
of all the top fighters –
including Hulk Hogan.

'He's the complete wrestler.
He's got all the moves.'

What is the secret of The Rock's success?

'It's a show,' he explains, 'first and last.
It's a soap-opera;
a physical soap-opera.
It's all about entertaining the fans.
If you forget the fans, they'll soon forget you!'

'The Rock' is also a movie star.
He's been in two blockbuster movies.

The Mummy Returns
was so popular,
'The Rock' made a prequel,
The Scorpion King.

10 Divas

There was a Women's Champion back in the 1950s.
Fabulous Moolah was queen of the scene
for an amazing 25 years.

Back in those days,
the matches could be a bit boring.
The women didn't have the skill, the power
or the passion they have today.

Even in the 1990s, women wrestlers
were still getting their act together.
At times it was a bit of a joke.

In one match,
a diva called 'The Kat'
lost her champion's title to a man in drag!

It wasn't until 2000
that women's wrestling grew up.

Trish Stratus.

New stars were on the scene.
Women like Lita, Jazz, Chyna and Ivory.
They looked good.
They put on a good show.
They actually knew how to wrestle.

In fact, Chyna got bored just fighting other women.
She was the first diva to take on the men – and win!

Women's wrestling came of age with Trish Stratus.

Trish Stratus started out
as Vince McMahon's girlfriend.
But she's not just a pretty face.

She fought her way to the top in record time.
She fought hard to win the Women's Title.
She fought hard to hold on to it.

She's a fighter. She'll never say die.

Along with Trish,
girls like Angel,
Stacy Keibler and Torrie Wilson
bring a bit of glamour to the ring.

11 You Think it's Not for Real?

Of course wrestling is not for real.
It's all fake. It's all staged.
The wrestlers don't really get hurt.

That's what some people say.

Here are some famous wrestlers who don't agree:

'I broke my nose twice.
I lost seven teeth.
I broke my jaw, a toe,
my wrist and my thumb.
Oh yes, and I lost half my right ear!'
(Mick 'Mankind' Foley)

'My neck hurts every single day.
I can't look to my left for too long.
The whole of the back of my head hurts.'
(Jazz)

'I fell badly on my arm.
I knew it was broken.

It didn't hurt,
but I knew there was something wrong.'
(Chris Jericho)

'This is a very tough game.
If you want to be in it,
you make your way through the pain.'
(Triple H)

'I broke my collar bone and wrist
falling out of the ring.
I was surprised it hurt so much
because it's only blood . . .'
(Mick McManus)

'He threw me out of the ring,
and I landed on something sharp.
I got eight stitches
and I lost a pint and a half of blood.
It was just spurting.
A man in the front row had a heart attack.'
(Mal Sanders)

You think wrestling is not for real?
Of course it's for real.